All These Little Remonstrations

poems by

Aurore Sibley

Finishing Line Press
Georgetown, Kentucky

All These
Little Remonstrations

Copyright © 2021 by Aurore Sibley
ISBN 978-1-64662-683-0 First Edition
All rights reserved under International and Pan-American Copyright Conventions. No part of this book may be reproduced in any manner whatsoever without written permission from the publisher, except in the case of brief quotations embodied in critical articles and reviews.

ACKNOWLEDGMENTS

"The Birth of Venus" appeared in *The Poeming Pigeon: The Cosmos Issue*, published by The Poetry Box, February, 2020

"All These Little Remonstrations" appeared in the *2018 Molotov Cocktail Prize Winners Anthology*, Volume 4, Copywright 2019, Accelerant Publishing, Portland, Oregon

"Someone Asked Me Why I Wore Black" appeared in *Women Who Roar: Still Healing*, Vol. 4, April 2019

"Whale Bone," "All These Little Remonstrations" and "The Orionids" were included in Black Mountain Press and The Halcyone's *The Sixty Four Best Poets of 2019*, published November, 2020

"May I Be Like the Ranunculus in Its Prime" is forthcoming in *The Paddock Review*, published by Finishing Line Press

Publisher: Leah Huete de Maines
Editor: Christen Kincaid
Cover Art: Aurore Sibley
Author Photo: Aurore Sibley
Cover Design: Elizabeth Maines McCleavy

Order online: www.finishinglinepress.com
also available on amazon.com

Author inquiries and mail orders:
Finishing Line Press
PO Box 1626
Georgetown, Kentucky 40324
USA

Table of Contents

The Birth of Venus 1

Sometime, 2020 2

May I Be Like the Ranunculus in Its Prime 3

Sunrise 4

The Cow Crab 5

My Father and The Civil War 6

My Daughter's Horn 8

For the Love of Food 9

Wings 10

My Dad Says 11

Fire Burns at the End of the World 12

The Orionids 13

All These Little Remonstrations 14

Whale Bone 15

Snowflakes and Spittle Bugs 16

Onions 17

Dark Pathways 18

Someone Asked Me Why I Wore Black 19

Online Dating for Single Mothers 20

A Safe Distance 21

Modern Romance 22

A Window 23

Walking the Heart Muscle 24

There are Three Kinds of Love, Perhaps,
    I've Been Studying Them 25

Four-leaf Clover 26

The Accident 27

Namesake 28

Stranger from Another World 30

The Birth of Venus

True, she's wearing nothing, but
even the breezes attend to her,
she is sea foam and innocence,
and everything draws gently towards her,
the flowered cloak and falling roses, wind and
sea and sky and stone, the sturdy porcelain of
the clamshell, the soft curve of the olive leaf—
but for all that, she looks inward, hand on her heart,
as if remembering what was, and contemplating
her absolute aloneness, now that she has come to Earth

Sometime, 2020

The poppies are all aflame this morning,
crowded like laughing girls against the
backdrop of the sand and salt water.
People don't stand so close together now,
we follow the rules, social distance with masks—
the way the crabs crawl under shells and rocks,
hiding their faces. You can still smell the moisture
of the sea air, just a little, through the filter of cloth,
and you can still tell when someone's eyes are smiling.

The flowers don't notice the difference, they
lean into each other and whisper, the sun
insists upon warming the spaces between us,
no matter how many feet wide, and the birds
swoop and dive all the same. Even the dogs
pull longingly at their leashes towards each other,
while the owners tug back gently and say, "No."

May I Be Like the Ranunculus in Its Prime

The other flowers bowed
with the weight of the raindrops,
but the ranunculus, with its
dancer's posture, raised its head
to the downpour—all color,
its graceful stem undaunted.
It weathered the onslaught of
the unexpected and glistened, its
beauty intensified, spotlighted,
as it stood so tall and quiet and proud.

Sunrise

I like the quiet of the early mornings, when the only stirrings are the cat's nuzzled demands and the singing of birds, and the children are still sleeping, so lovely in their rest, and the moon smiles from its perch and the dawn stretches herself, spreading color across the sky, light rising like music.

The Cow Crab

The tide was out so we rolled up our jeans, dipped our toes
into cold saltwater. At first, we found the little things,

barnacles and shells, fossils embedded in the rocks.
We buried your feet in the sand and searched for sea stars,

our little collection of polished treasures multiplied,
soon filling the canvas bag we'd brought along.

I went tide pooling with my father once, and found a
perfect sand dollar—I still have it, sitting on a shelf at home.

I would have liked for you to meet your grandfather, but flesh
and living things pass away, while stones and shells will stay.

It was you who found the cow crab, incomplete but
larger than my hand, his shell ridged with boney growths,

dense protrusions. You could still make his mouth move,
the sinews of his jaw and palate and eyes intact.

He must've been a hundred years, he must have been
older than my father, who was only sixty-five.

We brought it home and cleaned it, put it next to the
sand dollar, where it will stay and stay and stay.

My Father and The Civil War

Cyrus Nicodemus Smith shot his daughter's eye out with a bb gun.
It was an accident, and she was called one-eyed Suzie after that.
Cyrus fought in the civil war. He took a bullet to his forehead, survived.
A surgeon dug out it and my father kept it in a safety deposit box
at the bank. It's our oldest family heirloom.

My father kept a bookshelf dedicated to The Civil War, and he could tell
you anything you want to know about the battle of this or that.
When I was growing up, our family vacations consisted of road trips
to civil war battlefield reenactments. I got to be a page boy once,
and run back and forth across a field of gunfire on both sides,
dodging blanks and carrying sealed communications in costume.
It was our idea of fun.

My father was a Yankee through and through. My brother was given the
solemn name of Carl Abraham, after the poet and the president.
They called my father zany, unusual, but I admired his quirks and was
proud of his eccentricities. In fact, his parents wanted to lock him up
when he was seventeen because he had long hair and listened to that
crazed poet, Dylan, and maybe also because they saw what was
coming, something unhinged, something he couldn't conquer,
something that drowned him in the end.

When he was a boy, my father would frequently faint when running
or doing farm chores. It was his job to mild the cows at both sunrise
and sunset. He was not talented at sports, he tripped and stumbled,
he collapsed. When he was twelve, they discovered a sizable hole
in his heart and my grandfather risked the farm to pay for the operation,
although the doctors pronounced that he would not live beyond
the age of thirty-five. In fact, he lived to be sixty-five,
and did not die of heart failure.

No, he was a survivor—of pulmonary thrombosis and high blood
pressure, heart attacks and stroke, possible frontal-temporal dementia,
homelessness and full breakdown psychosis; it was lymphoma
in the end. My brother told me that when the doctor recommended

radiation and chemotherapy, but told him that it might kill my father,
and that the cancer certainly would anyway, my father threw back
his head and laughed, his hearty, cackling, roaring guffaw
coming out like a frog's croak for the lump in his throat.

When my father was six years old he was sent to live in an orphanage
for a year, after his mother lost her ability to walk from myasthenia
gravis and his father fought to save the family farm. She saw a famous
chiropractic doctor and became one of his early miracles, regaining
her stride, albeit with a cane. My father and his two sisters
returned home and the farm lasted another six years, until the state
of Illinois forced them off of it to build an interstate highway.

Still, he was the first black sheep in the family since Cyrus, who was
always drunk and shot his daughter's eye out, though my father
detested guns unless they had anything to do with the civil war.
He loved the curious and the strange, the quirky and unusual.
He threw his opinions around like sparks and I woke up every
morning of my early life to the sound of him talking back to the
radio host on NPR and conversing with the cat.
They, at least, understood one another.

I have his eyes, everyone tells me,
and I throw my head back when I laugh out loud,
the way he used to do.

My Daughter's Horn

We stopped in for cheesecake, maybe mousse,
a New Orleans style jazz band was playing and
we sat outside the widow, listening, watching through the glass.
I told her about the trombone, the way it sulks and murmurs,
and the soprano saxophone's clear tone,
I explained to her about the trumpet, all brass and shine,
the bass violin and the banjo.
There was a piano player and I listened closely to his solos,
my fingers aching slightly, reminiscing.
It was cold outside and she wanted a better look at that
trumpet and his muffler, so we went inside.
I stood at the back of the room, she edged closer,
curled herself up under the bar's ledge and cozied up underneath
the trombone's simper. She didn't hear me call her,
was riveted. They played Basin Street Blues and I thought of
my father who played this music for me and loved this music,
who would have beamed at this band and the café crowd.
She sat and listened, transfixed. Finally, she turned and ran over
to me, crawled into my lap and leaned back, and I asked her
Which instrument do you want to play?

For Love of Food

When things were going well, he made Jambalaya,
experimental pad Thai, got creative with pancakes.
The kitchen was a place of laughter, the radio blared,
there were hot dishes and Mexican hot chocolates.

If there was only Campbell's soup or frozen
TV dinners with the news blaring while we ate,
it meant something altogether different,
a mother tight-lipped but quietly resigned

while hunching over a barely balanced checkbook,
it meant an hour cutting coupons from the Sunday paper,
it meant perhaps another job had been lost, perhaps
another move across the country was impending,

or the dreaded word, *divorce*.
Maybe it was why I turned away from things not homemade,
why I shun store-bought meals and packaged, frozen foods,
why big brand sales make me cringe.

If he didn't make it and put some love into it
it was not food, it was only a hint that another
low had been hit, it was a foretelling of
days spent lying on the couch doing nothing.

When he moved away to find work in another state,
we ate hamburger helper every night,
there was a freezer full of chicken pot pies and
TV dinners, because my mother did not cook.

Wings

It is Monterey in March, and the bench lies
underneath the canopy of butterflies,

the limbs of the eucalyptus heavy
with their ethereal weight. Hundreds dance

in the sun's rays while my mother lays dozing on the bench,
looking up through sleepy, heavy-lided eyes.

They land on her, lightly, like a flower.
Every year she made the pilgrimage to see them—

I like to think of her there, her hair still black,
the future decades still spreading hopefully forward.

Back then, she had just one weekend to herself
each year,—I know now what that means,

being a single mother of two myself.
She raised us while working more than full time,

while supporting my father, who I adored,
but who could not find his backbone, or hold a job.

Once, in Monterey, she fell asleep on the bench and
awoke to four deer resting in a circle around her

underneath the canopy of flowers, with the salt air
and the butterflies, and the afternoon sun's golden shimmer.

I don't know how she did it sometimes—those moments
must have kept her going, while her teenage daughter

back at home couldn't yet grasp what it meant to be a
woman, didn't yet know that the magic of a moment

could keep your tired wings in flight, could lift
a gentle warrior, for that is what a mother is.

My Dad Says

My dad said if Dylan
pissed in a bottle and
played a toothpick
he would buy the album.

My dad said, why didn't
someone just shoot him?
I didn't like to hear him
say it, but it was after
he was already gone.

He told my brother and me
that there was only one thing
in his life that he did right,
which was us. But that's two.

My dad said *what happened
to me?* and I did not have the
answer. The last year he did not
say anything at all. My dad said

*you are the golden girl and
the world is your oyster*, he said
cats should run for government—
it would be an improvement,

he said, *listen to this* and played
I Shall Be Released. He said
I was lucky that I had inherited
nothing from him but his eyes.

Fire Burns at the End of the World

Once, we were driving past a field
that caught fire—maybe someone had
flung a cigarette out of the window,
the flames spread in seconds, consuming
the dry blades of grass and spreading
across the field like a scream, hot
tongues and sparks and black smoke.

We stopped at the closest house and
dialed 911—(this was before cell phones).
The sirens came and the fire was
contained. There was little devastation,
no real loss, but for a field of dry grass
along the highway. Nowadays the flames
chase people from their homes and feast,
leaving conduits of terror in their wake.

California is on fire—the golden state is red
and black and singed and the scent of
eucalyptus has been replaced with soot and
smoke and fire retardant. October leaves,
safe flames of orange and yellow, are now
charred and ash, and the sunsets have gone red,
and the fire was never so hungry.

Does the fire take its cue from us—who
cannot put down our virtual worlds and
single use plastics, except when they need
to be replaced, thrown away, discarded,
because there is always more, because
is climate change real?—because we treat
it all as if it were so very expendable,
as if it will always be there for us tomorrow.

The Orionids

I would like to know what it's like, to fall into your arms,
I imagine it would feel like a blanket of grass, like the sun
warming skin, like moonlight kissing eyelids,

I imagine it would feel like home. I keep digging
into the bold places in my body that might muster
the courage to ask you—would you?

Tonight the Orionids are spinning upside down and across the sky,
belly dancing their way to invisible realms. When a star dies,
it shines. Sometimes when I see you, I feel a little of that inevitable

sparkle, beckoning like a last dance home—
it would feel like the swell of the sea at low tide,
or maple sugar melting on my tongue,

and I imagine that you might be looking up at the stars,
too, that they might remind you of my eyes
when you see me looking at you.

All These Little Remonstrations

Winged things have always visited me. There was the
fledgling robin who'd fallen from his nest—we made a bed
for it in a shoebox, gave him worms and water.
He either mended and flew away one day, or our parents
removed him before we could see—I do not know which,

and there was the brown bat who'd inured his wing in
a sudden thunderstorm, I tried, but how could a brown bat
fathom that my gloved hands wanted to stall death? I'd
only imagined that he could sip water from a tea saucer,
that my remonstrations could change his longevity.

And when I asked for help, there was the hummingbird
with its honeyed needle of a beak, and
when I asked for a miracle, there was the hawk
with its precision of flight.

What I like about birds and flying things—they always sing
the truth, I believed you when you said this was something
to be counted on—like the certainty of seeing
the turkey vultures circling above the hills in Big Sur,
always and again, intent, so that

when you changed your mind without explanation, it was
like that time that a red-tailed hawk fell out of the sky
and dead at my feet. I was standing at a bus stop
on a busy San Francisco street corner,
and it made no sense.

It was so beautiful, but there were no remonstrations
my hands could perform, no song I could sing,
that would bring it back to life.

Whale Bone

Sometimes the loneliness is a bone,
like one of those rare whalebones you might find
on the ocean shore, hollowed out and polished
by wind and sea and sand, perfectly stark and beautiful,

usually the children need to be at baseball practice
and there is dinner to be made and the groceries bought,
the dog needs a walk and there are bedtime stories and baths,
usually the quiet is kept at bay with NPR and lesson planning,

there are birthday parties and the common cold,
a good book to read, and the day is full of children and
so many checks on the to-do lists waiting to be writ,
there are emails to respond to, utilities to pay,

there are my daughter's braids to brush out and her smile,
and the demands of another meal, there are the rare moments—
maybe half an hour—for a daydream, and the even exhale of a day
well spent, there is Masterpiece Mystery—and

sometimes the wind creeps up like it does at the sea,
it comes up from behind and blows you over and
the ache of the cold is a sneaker wave you couldn't brace against,
and the tears are all salt and no water

Snowflakes and Spittle Bugs

My daughter knows how to find the spittle bug in its moist home,
hiding in its nest of bubbles and spit. She finds the secrets
in most things, climbs to the tallest branches that she can reach
in the old oak, that are still within the bounds of safe.

The other day she asked me if boys can go shirtless, why can't she?
I didn't know how to answer her. I cannot tell her about all the
myriad of things that can live in the world and in men, not yet.

She does not question why I am alone, why a mother should or
Should not have love in her life. She looks at the flowers and she
says, *look, mommy, how beautiful the world is,* and I agree with her.

I would ask her one, like I would ask you, whether she
ever gets the feeling that we're all just snowflakes
seeking the soft bed of the ground? There might be a kind
of love there if we can settle into it without melting.

There are nights when loneliness washes over me like the swell
of a high tide and I wonder what it would be like, to have
that kind of love in my life. But tonight, as I was tucking her in,
my daughter hugged me and said, *mommy, the whole world
loves you,* and I knew that she was right.

Onions

If my mind drifts while cooking dinner, or during some other
whimsical, vulnerable moment, I push it aside
with the chopped onions.

There isn't space to miss you—what would be the point?
I am here, and you are somewhere else,

and if I eat a little too fast or a little too much,
it's not for want of company—is it?
Eating is a social art.

The problem is that you wanted to be free without allowing me
that same freedom—as if it was something you
had the right to determine,

and the funny thing is, you probably each think this poem
is about you, don't you? When in reality it's about myself,
and the lack of any man in my life.

There is no partner, no other half, no love of my life,
no prince charming—that's a myth for sure and
thank goodness, because I make
a better happy ending to my own day.

And if I miss you, I throw the chopped onions
into the boiling water.

Dark Pathways

Sometimes I wonder about the neuroplasticity of things,
you know, the way our minds can think

and then think again. We're so good at feeding the
amygdala—fear is everywhere and easy to divulge,

distraction has become a modern art form, compulsions
are encouraged: fortnite, google, sugar, French fries,

but when I was eighteen, before cell phones were
a commonality, I spent a summer on a small farm

where it was my job to pick the basil in the mornings,
and the zinnias and the sunflowers, and the scent would seep

into my hair and skin and my feet would sink into the soil,
and summer thunderstorms were the main entertainment.

There was an abandoned train track that ran along the perimeter
of the farm, and a long, curving tunnel, maybe half a mile,

all graffitied and crumbling, and we would walk through it
on an afternoon, navigating without flashlight or GPS,

our steps curving along the tracks and the damp, stone walls
a cool respite from the muggy weather, and only our senses

to guide us. I would like to disconnect from the shackles of wifi
again and go back in time to where only the cicadas can call me

Someone Asked Me Why I Wore Black

To be brief, I'll give you ten reasons,

    1.   The first kiss. It was "only a kiss."
He pushed me against a wall while his friend laughed, and
I Did Not want to kiss anyone again for a very long time.

    2.   For when he locked me in a room and said
he would not hurt me if I complied.

    3. and 4. For the boyfriends that took their liberties without consent.

    5.   For the doctor who assaulted me in his office. I bled for two weeks.

    6.   Because I was made to hug most of my assailants *after* their assault.

    7. Because I Never. Reported. Any of them. Because My Shame was too great to fathom speaking it.

    8. Because blood does not show up on black.

    9. Nor other bodily fluids, not so much.

    10. Because black is the color of mourning.

Online dating for single mothers

First, answer the questions, they help you match up
with potential mates. You can weed out the playboy/
looking for hookups type pretty quick, admire a photo
and move on. You've waited so long to join the bandwagon,
evenings always busy with bath and story time, tentative about
putting yourself out there, because you're not just one person, and,
you think, who would want to date a full-time single mother?

Let me tell you, you'll get seventy likes in the first hour, and
you might find one or two that you could like back;
you think it will take some time and it feels a little like
online shopping: which is the best product, the best deal?
You'll find the man that is perfect in so many ways, but who
wants more of your time than you can give, or the man
who beckons with the allure of attraction and adventure,
but already raised his children and doesn't want more,
maybe you'll make a friend, and whatever happens, it sure is
entertaining, and an investment of time. And whatever

happens, you go home to your children and tuck them in,
stroke their heads at bedtime and wonder how you
could introduce another human into your home life,
how it could all fit together, how the men without children
would ever adjust, or the men with children could ever commit,
or whether you could ever be alluring enough for a man
to fall in love with not just you, but all three of you.

A Safe Distance

I like to keep things at arm's length,
   —that is to say, that is where
I have the most control,
   I can pull something close
or I can push it away—
   I can keep it right where it is.

So often things are out of reach,
   or uncomfortably close,
inaction is not beguiling, but
   I like to keep things at arm's length,
—there is no commitment then, you see,
   there is just possibility.

I like to maneuver things
   with my own hands,
it could go either way—I could be brave
   and reach, or I could let it go,
there is opportunity, there is freedom,
   —I want to keep you at arm's length.

Modern Romance

The way I see it, we fill something for each other, you say,
and it's true, I haven't been lonely since we started,

you even blow me a kiss every morning by emoji,
that's modern love, you say. It's really hard

to find someone that you gel with, you say,
nothing's perfect, you say. We want different things,

I say. We all want something, you say. It's like wearing
a gardening glove that's a little too tight, I say,

it fits too loose, you say. In the greenhouse
where you work, there are aphids that love the plant,

but they love it too much, engulfing its stem,
eating away at its vitality with lust.

We all have our baggage, I say. But you can't
deal with mine, you say, and again you speak truth.

I was falling in love with you, you say, but in the greenhouse
you plant the beneficiaries and set loose the predatory

pests, you spray them with rosemary and lemon oil,
for it is your position to control what threatens,

to kill to sustain—you do this, to save the plant—I
love you, you say, but you say it by emoji in a text,

and I keep looking at it and wondering if you will
understand that it is my love that speaks when I say goodbye.

A Window

Through the window I see you sitting there. There's probably an open bottle of ten-dollar wine on the table, a coffee mug leftover from the morning. Maybe you're pacing, probably you're hunched over your phone, or a painting that you've been working on. You've smoked too much weed today, and you've watched a lot of Youtube. Maybe the painting is your fourth version of the same face, each rendition darker than the last. Maybe she has black hair now, maybe she was blonde. Maybe she has my eyes, or maybe yours. It doesn't matter. Whatever you paint looks good, and the colors are startling. You ignore the incoming text notifications and the sounds of traffic. The light is wintery and gold. Dylan or some other bard is spinning tales while you lounge and labor. And there is the wine and there is the bong. And there are the banished lovers and there are the Instagram women and there is your easle, and what more do you care to need?

Walking the Heart Muscle

I went for a walk, not to escape, but to search for understanding.

I think I can't write about love anymore, but there's nothing else
to write about. It is the love of the wind that bends the blades of grass,
it is the sun that illuminates the dirt path, so that it almost shimmers,

and what is the sun, but love? I wonder sometimes how human beings
cannot love each other more, how nature, too, can go from nurture
to condemn. Does a thunderstorm love? Does it express its depth of

feeling by beating down on Earth, shouting out its anger like a gunshot?
And when the sky withholds its water, is it to lovingly teach us that it is
our need that is our failing? I like to think that moments of wonder beget

love, that small gestures of care fold into the fabric of things—the beetle
turned over with a twig so that it can scuttle away, the bee rescued from the
water with cupped hands while knowing it might sting—the giving of

something small to someone who sees what was little to us, as tremendous.
So are lesser hurts, though we forget how the shrug of a shoulder, the silence
of pride, the slash of sarcasm—can wound, how salt can be rubbed into an

invisible fissure. How gentle things can turn to violence. And because
the heart yearns to expand, I go for walks and watch the wind as it
bends the trees' limbs and the birds that soar in their graceful arcs,
and I breathe the scent of jasmine

and bay leaves, and it almost comforts the stinging—the sun and the dirt
of the Earth almost begin to mend the bruises in that tender, fierce muscle,
the heart. It doesn't mean I understand, it only means
that I find solace in the quiet things that speak of love.

There are three kinds of love, perhaps, I've been studying them

One is the flood. It is a kind of light. It is difficult to see anything else when it shines. Sometimes that's okay, and sometimes it blinds.

One is a slow burn, very pleasant. Sometimes it smokes and bothers, it has to work hard to sustain itself, usually it surprises.

And there is the kind that just is, that doesn't require anything of you and that you do not require. But when it blossoms, we are better for it,

And the world is better, too.

Four-leaf Clover

I looked and looked and looked
for a four-leaf clover—I really tried,
maybe I tried half-heartedly.
There's a sea of them, clovers
everywhere you gaze, in the cracks
along the sidewalk, by the riverbed,
in the meadow. They all look the same,
little trinities of double-green leaves,
and they often trick you into thinking
that this one could be a lucky four-leaf,
a one of a kind—waiting for you to find it.

Maybe it's okay to miss them again and again,
maybe the ones I've chosen were spurious.
I know they exist—some people find them,
some people have that knack, and I keep
searching and hoping, even though I know
that it's when you're not looking that
you find what you're seeking, even though
maybe the four-leaf clover has been there
all along, and I just didn't recognize it,
patiently waiting in the shadows.

The Accident

There was the before and there was the after, metal stretched thin and
metal bruised, forced into an accordion wailing a dissonant cord,
the simple moment that the tires spun, three circles, and just
enough time to register disbelief, there was the spinning—an extended
moment in time, and the sudden loss of control, so unexpected
and dizzying, a blind spot.

There was the slam into cement and the airbags punching my face,
and a screeching of metal thrown across two lanes and backwards into
a second cement barrier, the force snapping vertebrae out of whack,
there was the cognitive registration that I was still alive, and that
the car was filling with smoke and something chemical.

Before the accident, the stress of little things added up—I moved too
quickly, worried about whether to let you know that I might love you,
about whether or not you might feel the same. Now it doesn't matter
because we're all just wind and rain and earth and sky and here
but for a moment and but for the blessing of another chance,
and I am no longer afraid because the fear was slammed out of me
at fifty or sixty miles an hour against a cement wall that was
unforgiving of metal and glass but spared my body, just.

In the aftermath of physical pain and restricted movement and the
knowledge that I was so very lucky, that I dumbfounded
the onlookers as I stepped out of the wreck of metal and smoke
into the drizzle of rain, I realize that my fears or expectations
are just water gushing past. You'll love me if you love me.

In real life there is only the ebb and flow of the heart's beat and our
breath and the simultaneous calm and agitation that I feel
when I am in your presence, and it is the warmth in our smiles
and the light in our eyes that reach across the barriers of what if's
and reaffirms that we will be fine no matter what, and that right
now is always the only moment that matters.

Namesake

It makes sense—
George was someone
who wore men's clothing
and bent the rules,

she loved and she
loved and she
smoked cigarettes,
wrote racy novels

that were more than loosely
based on her own life and
the lives of her lovers.
Sometimes it's difficult to

live up to the image
of someone who wanted
to be like a man, yet loved
like a woman. She tended

to Chopin, adored and challenged
him, lay under his piano
while they both made their art,
and despite their differences

that is what remains. I would
like to tell her that it is fine
to be a woman now—they
let us do the things she did

anyway, but the fact is that
they still try to make it
uncomfortable—and the lovers
still want so much of you,

and a woman is still
supposed to be so many
things—everything, really,
both a man and a woman,

at least that has been
my truth—father and mother
provider and nurturer,
bread winner and homemaker,

and yet I wouldn't have it
any other way. I like to
chose when I wear pants
or a skirt, and I cut my hair

just how I like it, and like
Madamme Sand, I am emboldened
to forge my own path and am
proud that it is not like any other.

Stranger from Another World

There was a beached whale on the shore this morning, with a row
of teeth and a white belly, marbled markings around its lifeless eye.
My daughter spotted it first, waved us over, gesticulating with
excitement, "Come here, quick, Mama! You've got to see this!"
The children stretched out next to it, measured its length against theirs,
noted its wounds, marveled at its strangeness and size.
It was a small whale, and blood still oozed from deep gashes in its side.

There are not many toothed whales in the Monterey Bay, more baleen,
this was not gray or humpback, blue or orca, it came from
deeper waters, somewhere unknown, some world away from our world
of grass and cars, washed up on our little beach, mortally stranded
but not yet decaying, its eye a glassy emptiness, its skin so smooth
and full, but marked with scars, like it had been through a few things,
and its teeth were so fine and small, sharp and curious.

I wished the water would lap at it and we could watch it roll over
and swim away, back into a place where we could never follow.
Forensics said it was a pigmy sperm whale, unusual and rare,
from deep, far-away waters. It had probably been dead a while,
pulled in by the tide, rolled and tossed by
the waves from an unknown ocean canyon
until it came to rest on our little stretch of sand,
a stranger from another world.

Aurore Sibley is a writer, musician, educator and healing arts professional living in California with her two children. *All These Little Remonstrations* is her second short poetry collection. She has been a contributing writer to *The Idea Crucible* and *Lilipoh* magazine, and her poetry and prose have appeared in numerous online and print publications, including *The Molltov Cocktail Award Anthology*. In the summer of 2020, Aurore released a self-produced album of original music, *Book of Song*, which can be found on all streaming platforms. Aurore is currently very busy taking her puppy on long walks and to the park, but a mystery novel is in the works. More information about her writing and music can be found at http://www.auroresibley.com

www.ingramcontent.com/pod-product-compliance
Lightning Source LLC
LaVergne TN
LVHW041510070426
835507LV00012B/1467